WHITEWASH

by Gabriel Bisset-Smith

SAMUEL FRENCH

samuelfrench.co.uk

FOR AMATEUR PRODUCTION ENQUIRIES

UNITED KINGDOM AND WORLD
EXCLUDING NORTH AMERICA
plays@samuelfrench.co.uk
020 7255 4302/01

Each title is subject to availability from Samuel French, depending upon country of performance.

THINKING ABOUT PERFORMING A SHOW?

There are thousands of plays and musicals available to perform from Samuel French right now, and applying for a licence is easier and more affordable than you might think

From classic plays to brand new musicals, from monologues to epic dramas, there are shows for everyone.

Plays and musicals are protected by copyright law, so if you want to perform them, the first thing you'll need is a licence. This simple process helps support the playwright by ensuring they get paid for their work and means that you'll have the documents you need to stage the show in public.

Not all our shows are available to perform all the time, so it's important to check and apply for a licence before you start rehearsals or commit to doing the show.

LEARN MORE & FIND THOUSANDS OF SHOWS

Browse our full range of plays and musicals, and find out more about how to license a show

www.samuelfrench.co.uk/perform

Talk to the friendly experts in our Licensing team for advice on choosing a show and help with licensing

plays@samuelfrench.co.uk   020 7387 9373

Acting Editions

BORN TO PERFORM

Playscripts designed from the ground up to work the way you do in rehearsal, performance and study

---

Larger, clearer text for easier reading

Wider margins for notes

Performance features such as character and props lists, sound and lighting cues, and more

---

+ CHOOSE A SIZE AND STYLE TO SUIT YOU

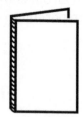

STANDARD EDITION

Our regular paperback book at our regular size

SPIRAL-BOUND EDITION

The same size as the Standard Edition, but with a sturdy, easy-to-fold, easy-to-hold spiral-bound spine

LARGE EDITION

A4 size and spiral bound, with larger text and a blank page for notes opposite every page of text – perfect for technical and directing use

LEARN MORE | **samuelfrench.co.uk/actingeditions**

MUSIC USE NOTE

Licensees are solely responsible for obtaining formal written permission from copyright owners to use copyrighted music in the performance of this play and are strongly cautioned to do so. If no such permission is obtained by the licensee, then the licensee must use only original music that the licensee owns and controls. Licensees are solely responsible and liable for all music clearances and shall indemnify the copyright owners of the play(s) and their licensing agent, Samuel French, against any costs, expenses, losses and liabilities arising from the use of music by licensees. Please contact the appropriate music licensing authority in your territory for the rights to any incidental music.

USE OF COPYRIGHT MUSIC

A licence issued by Samuel French Ltd to perform this play does not include permission to use the incidental music specified in this copy.

Where the place of performance is already licensed by the PERFORMING RIGHT SOCIETY (PRS) a return of the music used must be made to them. If the place of performance is not so licensed then application should be made to the PRS, 2 Pancras Square, London, N1C 4AG. www.prsformusic.com

A separate and additional licence from PHONOGRAPHIC PERFORMANCE LTD, 1 Upper James Street, London W1F 9DE (www.ppluk.com) is needed whenever commercial recordings are used.

IMPORTANT BILLING AND CREDIT REQUIREMENTS

If you have obtained performance rights to this title, please refer to your licensing agreement for important billing and credit requirements.

For mum and dad.

ACKNOWLEDGMENTS

I pretty much did this on my own so... Joking! Every aspect of this play was a collaboration, but if I don't start by thanking my mum she'll fucking kill me. Thanks mum. For helping shape me, this play and all the amazing artwork you've done for it. Buy her art guys. Seriously.

Next up is my dad. Now he isn't present in the play but that's just a dramatic device, he was very present in real life and a lot of these stories are his too. He's the reason I can even write them. Love you dad, you are my hero.

I have to give a massive thanks to my director and friend Charlotte Bennett. She's believed and supported me throughout my career, and this play wouldn't exist without her. I can't stress enough how important she has been to my growth as a writer and performer, as well as a great friend (plus she introduced me to the North). Thank you Bennett.

Then there's the rest of my family, especially Ezra, Sol and Sarbjit. Again they are not in this story but that are definitely part of it. Love you all more than you will ever know.

Thank you Rebekah Murrell whose honesty and intelligence during rehearsals was incredible. Again this play would be nothing without you on board. From the very first reading, Charlotte and I knew there was no one else who could play this part.

Thank you to our wonderful creative team, and Francesca Moody, you are a star. Not only a wonderful friend, but a brilliant producer. Love you, bye!

I'd also like to say a huge thanks to the whole team at the Soho Theatre, especially David and Nadine. Soho have given me so much support over the years.

My agents Kat, Nish and Sam! You guys are the best.

Meghan Cruz and Molly Seymour, your tips for Personal Survival In The City have been life changing.

Oh and my girlfriend Hannah for just being around. Love you babe (you can't dump me now cause I've written this in a book).

And Andy Hui for helping with all my housing research and the many tenants who spoke with me and have been fighting for housing rights every day.

Now for all the people who gave their time and read many drafts. You legends. Phoebe Waller-Bridge, Vicky Jones, Matilda Ibini, Lainey Richardson, Rachel De-lahay, Danny Lee Wynter, Zawe Ashton, Gwilym Gold, Graham Turner, Kenny Emson, Deirdre O'Halloran, Lakesha Arie-Angelo, Alan Caroll, Polly Cavendish, Michael McCoy and I guess I should thank Robert Cawsey for something. Nah. Fuck you Rob.

Whitewash premiered at Soho Theatre on 3 July 2019, in a co-production between Francesca Moody Productions and Soho Theatre with the following cast and creatives:

CAST

LYSANDER	Gabriel Bisset-Smith
MARY	Rebekah Murrell

CREATIVES

Writer	Gabriel Bisset-Smith
Director	Charlotte Bennett
Set and Costume Designer	Jemima Robinson
Lighting Designer	Jai Morjaria
Composer	Asaf Zohar
Video Designer	Daniel Denton
Associate Video Designer	Barbora Šenoltová
Original Artwork	Jenny Gordon
Producer	Francesca Moody
Assistant Producer	Holly De Angelis
Stage Manager	Rachael Head
Production Manager	Seb Cannings
Casting Director	Nadine Rennie CDG

Supported by DryWrite
Special thanks to David Luff, Katie Posner and Mesmer

CAST AND CREATIVES

GABRIEL BISSET-SMITH
WRITER/PERFORMER (LYSANDER)

Gabriel Bisset-Smith is a BAFTA-nominated writer/actor/director/comedian.

He directed, co-created and co-wrote the BBC's groundbreaking multi-platform murder mystery, *The Last Hours of Laura K*, which earned him a BAFTA nomination in digital creativity. The show was also nominated for a Prix Italia, best visual experience at SXSW Interactive and won a Gold and Audience Award at the LOVIES as well as best Multi-Platform at the International Format Awards in Cannes. It was also nominated for a Broadcast Digital Award.

He wrote, directed and starred in his debut short film, *Thrush*, which won the Vimeo Best Narrative award. The following year he was asked to judge and present the same category. The film also won the Rushes Soho Shorts Festival Tenderpixel audience choice award and the Grand Jury Prize at the Disposable Film Festival. He was named one of Dazed & Confused Magazine's Dazed Visionaries and they commissioned him, alongside the likes of Becky & Joe and Bjork, to make his award-winning film *Toilets*.

Theatre credits include: his debut play, *The Charming Man*, which was nominated for the Off West End Most Promising Playwright Award, plays at Hampstead Theatre and York Theatre Royal and attachments at the Royal Court and the Soho Theatre. After taking part in the 24 Hour Plays at the Old Vic Theatre he was selected to workshop his play, *Dreams of a Butterfly Broker*, at The Public Theatre in New York. He also directed Jack Rooke's debut show *Good Grief,* which was nominated for Total Theatre award. For radio he wrote and starred in *The Black Bono*, BBC Radio Four.

Gabriel is a successful comedian and makes satirical online sketches which have raked up over a million views online and he has been commissioned by BBC Comedy to make some for their online platforms. His sketch, *Shy Corbynites*, was nominated for a Writers Guild of Great Britain Award.

His debut solo comedy hour *Gabriel Bisset-Smith Tells the Most Original and Funny Joke in the Universe* was produced by the Soho Theatre, received rave reviews at the Fringe and a sell-out run at the Soho Theatre. He is also one half of comedy double act GUILT & SHAME alongside Robert Cawsey. They have played sold-out shows at the Soho Theatre, Underbelly, Bestival, Latitude and currently have a podcast of the same name which they make with award-winning playwright and director Vicky Jones.

He was just named a Screen Star Of Tomorrow by Screen Daily Magazine.

REBEKAH MURRELL
MARY

Rebekah trained with the National Youth Theatre, Tricycle Young Company, The Actors Class and ALT. Her theatre work includes: Anita in the Olivier Award-nominated *Nine Night* (National Theatre and Trafalgar Studios); *The Host* (NYT); and *Puppy* (Vaults Festival). TV includes: *Being Victor*, *Myths*, and *The Roman Mysteries*. Radio includes: *The Gift*, for which she received a BBC Audio Drama Award 2018 nomination for Best Debut Performance.

As a director, her work includes: *J'Ouvert* (Theatre503) and *Interrupted* (JW3); and the short plays: *Stopcock* (Southwark Playhouse); *Do You Pray?* (Theatre503); *Red As Rubies* (Arcola Theatre); and *Long Walk From Home* (Lyric Hammersmith). She assisted on *We Too Are Giants* (Kiln Theatre) and *Black Lives Black Words* (Bush Theatre).

CHARLOTTE BENNETT
DIRECTOR

Charlotte is Associate Director at Soho Theatre and is the incoming Joint Artistic Director of Paines Plough Theatre Company.

Directing credits at Soho Theatre include: *Happy Hour* (Soho Theatre / Edinburgh Underbelly) and *The Turas Mor* (Soho Theatre at Lloyd Park Walthamstow).

Prior to this Charlotte was Artistic Director of Forward Theatre Project; an artists' collective she founded through which she directed new plays which toured nationally including: *Clothes Swap Theatre Party* (Derby Theatre); *Genesis* (The Lowry / Soho Theatre and tour); *On the Harmful Effects of Tobacco/ Can Cause Death* (National Theatre Cottesloe / Northern Stage) and *A Five-Star Werewolf* (York Theatre Royal).

Charlotte has worked extensively for Open Clasp Theatre Company directing new plays by Catrina McHugh MBE including: *Rattle Snake* (Live Theatre / Soho Theatre and tour); *The Space Between Us* (Live Theatre and tour) and *Swags and Tails* (Live Theatre and tour).

Charlotte also held the role of Producer for theatre company RashDash for four years, producing experimental new theatre around the UK and beyond and is a graduate of Hull University.

ASAF ZOHAR
COMPOSER

Asaf Zohar is a composer for theatre, film and television. His previous work includes scoring and performing in shows at Deptford Albany, Ovalhouse Theatre, Brighton Festival and Half Moon Theatre, with upcoming shows at Edinburgh Fringe and Birmingham Repertoire Theatre. Asaf has been commissioned to score numerous productions for BBC, Channel 4, and Virgin Media, amongst others. Asaf studied classical composition at the Royal College of Music after years of professionally playing rock guitar. He has written scores in a multitude of genres and forms on commission, while specialising in contemporary production techniques.

JAI MORJARIA
LIGHTING DESIGNER

Jai trained at RADA and won the 2016 Association of Lighting Designer's ETC Award.

Recent designs include: *Aesop's Fables* (Unicorn Theatre); *Mapping Brent* (Kiln Theatre); *Mary's Babies* (Jermyn Street Theatre); *Glory* (Duke's Theatre / Red Ladder); *Cuzco* (Theatre503); *The Hoes* (Hampstead Theatre); *Losing Venice* (Orange Tree Theatre); *King Lear, Lorna Doone* (Exmoor National Park); *Sufi:Zen* (Akademi Dance); *Superhero: The Musical* (NYMT); *Kanye the First* (HighTide); *Bitched* (Kali

Theatre); *A Lie of the Mind, A Midsummer Night's Dream* (Southwark Playhouse); *The Cunning Little Vixen* (Arcola Theatre / The Opera Company); *46 Beacon* (Trafalgar Studios with Rick Fisher); *Out There on Fried Meat Ridge Road* (White Bear Theatre / Trafalgar Studios 2); *Acorn* (Courtyard Theatre, Off West End Award nomination for Best Lighting) and *The Beggar's Opera, Pains of Youth, Obama-ology* (RADA).

www.jaimorjaria.com

JEMIMA ROBINSON
DESIGNER

Jemima was awarded the Max Rayne Design Bursary at the National Theatre which she completed in March 2018. Jemima is a winner of the biennial Linbury Prize for Stage Design 2011 and the Bristol Old Vic Technical Theatre award. She has been nominated for Best Set Design Off West End Awards for *Br'er Cotton* at Theatre 503 and for *Thebes Land* at the Arcola Theatre. Her design work has been exhibited at the National Theatre and Royal Festival Hall. She is a former resident artist at Kenya's Kuona Arts Trust in Nairobi and resident designer for Istanbul's Talimhane Theatre.

Current projects include: *Whitewash* (Soho Theatre); *Oedipus at Colonus* (Cambridge); *Cosi Fan Tutte* (Wales Millennium Centre) and *I'll Take You to Mrs Cole!* (Complicité)

Her recent design credits include: *The Trick* (Bush Theatre, UK Tour); *Keith?* (Arcola); *Twelfth Night* (Guangzhou Dramatic Arts Centre, China in collaboration with the Royal Shakespeare Company); *Playing with Scale* (National Theatre exhibition: Wolfson Gallery); *Hansel and Gretel* (Opera for Hidden Woods, Iford Arts); *Br'er Cotton* (Theatre 503, Nominated for Best Set Design for Off West End Awards); *The Majority* (Dorfman, National Theatre); *New Nigerians, Thebes Land* (Nominated for Best Set Design and Winner of Best Production for Off West End Awards); *Maria de Buenos Aires* (Arcola); *Parallel Yerma* (Young Vic); *License to Ill, This Will End Badly, Little Malcolm and his Struggle Against the Eunuchs* (Southwark Playhouse); *Biederman and the Arsonists, Synergies: Nebt* (Sadlers Wells); *Mapping Brent* (Tricycle Theatre); *Dyl, Sparks* (Old Red Lion); *Hearing Things* (Albany); *The Dark Room* (Theatre 503); *The Tempest* (Watermill Theatre) and *I Love You, You're Perfect, Now Change* (Zorlu Centre, Istanbul).

Jemima has also designed events, exhibitions, merchandise and foyers for the National Theatre, King's Cross Theatre and Waldorf Hotel. She has run workshops and worked on community projects for The Young Vic, Kiln Theatre (The Tricycle), Ilford Arts and the National Theatre.
www.jemimarobinson.com

DANIEL DENTON
VIDEO DESIGNER

Daniel Denton is a London-based Video Designer and Animator and associate of video design collective Mesmer. His background is in illustration and experimental film and to date has created visuals across theatre, opera, music, fashion and broadcast.

Design credits include: *Us Against Whatever* (Middle Child Theatre); *Flashdance: The Musical* (Korean Tour); *The Little Prince* (Protein Dance); *Sundowning* (Kali Theatre Company); *James Graham's: Sketching* (Wilton's Music Hall); *On Raftery's Hill* (Abbey Theatre); *Misty* (Bush Theatre and Trafalgar Studios); *As You Like It* (Theatre By the Lake); *Flashdance: The Musical* (UK and International Tour); *To Love Somebody Melancholy* (National Tour); *Ready or Not* (The Arcola Theatre and National tour); *Peter Pan* (Exeter Northcott Theatre); *Bumblescratch* (Adelphi Theatre) and *Biederman and the Arsonists* (Sadler's Wells).

NADINE RENNIE
CDG

Nadine has been Casting Director at Soho Theatre for over fifteen years; working on new plays by writers including Dennis Kelly, Vicky Jones, Phoebe Waller-Bridge, Roy Williams, Philip Ridley, Shelagh Stevenson, D C Moore, Alecky Blythe and Oladipo Agboluaje. Directors she has worked during this time include Rufus Norris, Tamara Harvey, Indu Rubasingham, Michael Buffong, Paulette Randall, Tim Crouch, Natalie Ibu, Roxana Silbert and Ellen McDougall. Freelance work includes BAFTA winning CBBC series *Dixi* (casting first three series). Nadine also has a long running association as Casting Director for Synergy Theatre Project and is a full member of the Casting Directors Guild.

FRANCESCA MOODY PRODUCTIONS

Francesca Moody Productions commissions, develops and presents brave, entertaining and compelling new theatre. They work with the UK's leading playwrights and discover and nurture new talent to produce bold, award-winning shows with universal appeal and commercial potential. Since launching in 2018 the company has been awarded two prestigious Fringe First Awards and has produced the critically-acclaimed *Angry Alan* by Penelope Skinner and *Square Go* by Kieran Hurley and Gary McNair in their world premieres at the Edinburgh Festival. In 2019 Francesca Moody productions will return to Edinburgh with two new productions, transfer work to New York, Dubai, London and tour across the UK.

Soho Theatre is London's most vibrant venue for new theatre, comedy and cabaret. We occupy a unique and vital place in the British cultural landscape. Our mission is to produce new work, discover and nurture new writers and artists, and target and develop new audiences. We work with artists in a variety of ways, from full producing of new plays, to co-producing new work, working with associate artists and presenting the best new emerging theatre companies that we can find.

We have numerous artists on attachment and under commission, including Soho Six and a thriving Young Company of writers and comedy groups. We read and see hundreds of scripts and shows a year.

'the place was buzzing, and there were queues all over the building as audiences waited to go into one or other of the venue's spaces....young, exuberant and clearly anticipating a good time.' Guardian.

We attract over 240,000 audience members a year at Soho Theatre, at festivals and through our national and international touring. We produced, co-produced or staged over 35 new plays in the last 12 months.

As an entrepreneurial charity and social enterprise, we have created an innovative and sustainable business model. We maximise value from Arts Council England and philanthropic funding, contributing more to government in tax and NI than we receive in public funding.

Registered Charity No: 267234

Soho Theatre, 21 Dean Street
London W1D 3NE
Admin 020 7287 5060
Box Office 020 7478 0100

OPPORTUNITIES FOR WRITERS AT SOHO THEATRE

We are looking for unique and unheard voices – from all backgrounds, attitudes and places.

We want to make things you've never seen before.

Alongside workshops, readings and notes sessions, there are several ways writers can connect with Soho Theatre. You can

Enter our prestigious biennial competition the **Verity Bargate Award** just as **Vicky Jones** did in 2013 with her Award-winning first play *The One*.

Participate in our nine month long **Writers' Labs programme**, where we will take you through a three-draft process.

Submit your script to submissions@sohotheatre.com where your play will go directly to our Artistic team

Or

Invite us to see your show via coverage@sohotheatre.com

We consider every submission for production or any of the further development opportunities.

sohotheatre.com

Keep up to date:

sohotheatre.com/mailing-list
@sohotheatre all social media

SUPPORTERS

PRINCIPAL SUPPORTERS
Nicholas Allott OBE
Hani Farsi
Hedley and Fiona Goldberg
Michael and Isobel Holland
Jack and Linda Keenan
Amelia and Neil Mendoza
Lady Susie Sainsbury
Carolyn Ward
Jennifer and Roger Wingate

SUPPORTING PARTNERS
Dean Attew
Jo Bennett-Coles
Tamara Box
Moyra Doyle
Stephen Garrett
Beatrice Hollond
Angela Hyde-Courtney
Dom & Ali Wallis
Garry Watts

CORPORATE SUPPORTERS
Adnams Southwold
Bargate Murray
Bates Wells & Braithwaite
Cameron Mackintosh Ltd
Character Seven
EPIC Private Equity
Financial Express
Fosters
The Groucho Club
John Lewis Oxford Street
Latham & Watkins LLP
Lionsgate UK
The Nadler Hotel
Oberon Books Ltd
Overbury Leisure
Quo Vardis
Richmond Associates
Soho Estates
Soundcraft

TRUSTS & FOUNDATIONS
The Andor Charitable Trust
The Austin and Hope
Pilkington Charitable Trust
Backstage Trust
Bertha Foundation
Bruce Wake Charitable Trust
The Boris Karloff Charitable
Foundation
The Boshier-Hinton
Foundation
The Buzzacott Stuart Defries
Memorial Fund
Chapman Charitable Trust
The Charles Rifkind and
Jonathan Levy Charitable
Settlement
The Charlotte Bonham-Carter
Charitable Trust
Cockayne – Grants for
the Arts and The London
Community Foundation
John S Cohen Foundation
The Coutts Charitable Trust
The David and Elaine Potter
Foundation
The D'Oyly Carte Charitable
Trust
The 8th Earl of Sandwich
Memorial Trust
The Edward Harvist Trust
The Eranda Rothschild
Foundation
The Ernest Cook Trust
Esmée Fairbairn Foundation
The Fenton Arts Trust
Fidelio Charitable Trust
The Foundation for Sport and
the Arts
Foyle Foundation
Garrick Charitable Trust
The Goldsmiths' Company
The Late Mrs Margaret
Guido's Charitable Trust
Harold Hyam Wingate
Foundation
Help A London Child
Hyde Park Place Estate
Charity
The Ian Mactaggart Trust
The Idlewild Trust
The John Thaw Foundation
John Ellerman Foundation
John Lewis Oxford Street
Community Matters Scheme
John Lyon's Charity
JP Getty Jnr Charitable Trust
The Kobler Trust
The Leche Trust
The Mackintosh Foundation
Mohamed S. Farsi Foundation
Noel Coward Foundation
The Peggy Ramsay
Foundation
The Rose Foundation
The Royal Victoria Hall
Foundation
Santander Foundation
Schroder Charity Trust
St Giles-in-the-Fields and
William Shelton Educational
Charity
The St James's Piccadilly
Charity
Tallow Chandlers Benevolent
Fund
The Teale Charitable Trust
The Theatres Trust
The Thistle Trust
Unity Theatre Charitable
Trust
The Wolfson Foundation

SOHO THEATRE PERFORMANCE FRIENDS
Matthew Bunting
Alban Gordon
Anya Hindmarch and James
Seymour
David King
Gary Kemp
Steve and Diane Kordas
Joe Lam
Andrew Lucas
Walter Ken McCracken and
Stacie Styles
Lady Caroline Mactaggart
Ian Ritchie and Jocelyne van
den Bossche
Mark Whiteley
Gary Wilder
Hilary and Stuart Williams
Patrick Woodroffe

SOHO THEATRE PLAYWRIGHT FRIENDS
David Aukin
Anthony Eaton
Denzil and Renate Fernandez
Emily Fletcher
Dominic Flynn
Liam Goddard
Andrew Gregory
Fawn James
John James
Shappi Khorsandi
Jeremy King OBE
David and Linda Lakhdhir
Jonathan Levy
David Macmillan
Phil and Jane Radcliff
Chantel Sinclair-Gray

Soho Theatre has the support of the Channel 4 Playwrights' Scheme sponsored by Channel 4 Television.

We are also supported by Westminster City Council West End Ward Budget and the London Borough of Waltham Forest.

We would also like to thank those supporters who wish to remain anonymous.

SOHO STAFF

Executive Director Mark Godfrey

Creative Director David Luff

BOARD OF DIRECTORS
Heather Rabbatts (chair)
Beatrice Hollond (vice chair)
Nicholas Allott OBE
David Aukin
Hani Farsi
Fawn James
Vicky Jones
Shappi Khorsandi
Jeremy King OBE
Kate Mayne
Carolyn Ward
Christopher Yu

HONORARY PATRONS
Peter Brook CBE
Simon Callow
Gurinder Chadha
Sir Richard Eyre CBE

ARTISTIC TEAM
Head of Comedy Steve Lock
Associate Director Charlotte Bennett
General Manager – Programme Rose Abderabbani
Associate Director Adam Brace
Touring Producer Sarah Dodd
Education Producer Jules Haworth
Comedy Associate Lee Griffiths
Casting Director Nadine Rennie
Associate Director Lakesha Arie-Angelo
Assistant Producer Holly De Angelis

ADMINISTRATION
Executive Assistant Laura Schofield
Financial Controller Kevin Dunn
Head of Finance & Administration Catherine McKinney
Finance Manager Olivier Pierre-Noel
Finance Assistant Niamh Caines
HR & Education Administrator Dimple Pau

DEVELOPMENT
Development Director Bhavita Bhatt
Development Manager Melanie Geelan
Development Assistant Beth Graham

COMMUNICATIONS
PR & Events Director Kelly Fogarty
Sales & Marketing Director Peter Flynn
Marketing Manager Sophie Coke-Steel
Press Officer Georgia Young
Marketing Officer Pete Simpson
Communications Officer Clare Nugent
Sales & Marketing Administrative Assistant Fuad Ahammed
Graphic Designer Conor Jatter

BOX OFFICE
Acting Sales & Box Office Manager Paul Carroll
Box Office Assistants Lainey Alexander, Gemma Leader, Emily Thomson, Kerry Taylor, Nancy Netherwood

OPERATIONS
Operations Director Julie Marshall
Deputy Front-of-House Manager: Hannah Horan
Duty and Venue Managers Rosina Acosta, Rachael Black, Thara Harrison, Rachael Smith, Ally Wilson
Head Ushers Sara Ferreira Sophy Plumb Cara Withers

FRONT OF HOUSE
Erol Arguden, Brenton Arrendell, Scott Barnett, Hamish Clayton, Naomi Denny, Rachel Gemaehling, Leonie Griffiths, Georgie King, James Kitching, Elspeth McColl, Katheryn Mather, George Nichols, Jim Robertson, Ariella Stoian, Ed Theakston, Jade Warner-Clayton, Toraigh Watson, Cara Withers,

PRODUCTION
Technical Manager Nick Blount
Head of Lighting Sean Hawkins
Head of Sound Paolo Carlotto
Senior Technician Paolo Melis
Technicians Kevin Millband, Georgina Trott
Freelance Technicians Scott Bradley, Branden Dukes, Hannah Fullelove

CHARACTERS

MARY
LYSANDER

All other parts to be played by **MARY** *and* **LYSANDER.**

SETTING

There should be a large brick wall painted white at the back of the stage. This will have images and videos projected on it throughout. Everything else should be minimal and white. Almost like a gallery space.

STYLING

/ means overlap

– means a quick follow on

Enter **MARY** *and* **LYSANDER***. She's in ripped jeans and a faded David Bowie T-shirt. He's in skinny fit jeans and a blazer.*

They both stare at the white wall, with their backs to us.

We hear a slightly muffled reggae beat, like it's coming from next door.

They turn to us.

LYSANDER Camden. 1989. And it is hot.

We now see images of Camden in the eighties on the wall. Punks smoking on corners, stylish black couples near Woolworths and Mods walking down the market...

MARY Really fucking hot. That inside-an-oven-hot you only get in a big concrete city.

LYSANDER You don't know where the sun ends, and the pollution begins. You can literally fry an egg on the pavement –

MARY – Fuck that, you can fry your whole breakfast. Eggs, sausages, bacon –

LYSANDER – Halloumi.

MARY*'s not impressed.*

MARY Music blares from every window. Car, home and shop.

The music becomes louder.

LYSANDER Reggae and Hip Hop intermingle to create a symphony of erratic beats and confused vibes.

MARY But the heat drowns them all out. Numbing your ears to the point of silence. Nothing can penetrate this thick hot fog. That's right –

BOTH – IT. IS. HOT.

LYSANDER A beautiful mixed-race woman, let's say twenty-four, nearly twenty-five –

MARY – Let's say twenty-four.

LYSANDER Walks hand in hand with a little boy. She's wearing a loose-fitting T-shirt that has Bowie's melancholy face printed on it, pouty and sad. Ripped denim jeans wrap around her long legs –

MARY – They are more circumstance than fashion.

LYSANDER Her hair is short, in an unpicked Afro –

MARY – More circumstance than fashion.

LYSANDER She's agitated. Only slightly but agitated none the less. Her name is Mary –

MARY – Not after the virgin, but the Tina Turner song.

LYSANDER She pulls the boy along faster than his little legs can carry him.

MARY Now the boy. The five-year-old boy.

LYSANDER He's white. Pretty fucking white.

MARY If he wore foundation his shade would be Casper. His hair is a mass of blond curls that nearly cover his sharp blue eyes. He's wearing a yellow T-shirt, which has something that strongly resembles strawberry ice-cream spilt down it –

LYSANDER – It was a strawberry Funny Feet.

We see an image of the strawberry Funny Feet ice cream.

MARY He pulls on Mary's hand like he's a monk ringing the bells of St Paul's. He wants something. Something in a shop window just passed.

LYSANDER A toy Castle Greyskull from the He-Man cartoons.

We see a clip of the Castle Greyskull advert.

What kid in the eighties didn't?

MARY But Mary doesn't have that kind of money. In fact, she doesn't have any kind of money. So, it was a hard no from her.

LYSANDER But the boy is not taking that for an answer.

MARY From the outside. From where we're looking right now, they make an unusual pair. Stark contrasts of colour, styles and directional desires.

LYSANDER And it may surprise you to know that they are indeed mother and son.

MARY Yep. Even Mary was surprised at how pale he came out.

LYSANDER And she has spent a large portion of his existence having to explain their connection.

MARY His dad's from Manchester.

LYSANDER And when they're out together she'll often get asked: Are you his nanny?

MARY Or:

LYSANDER Where are you taking him?

MARY Or:

LYSANDER If Lysander is stood crying next to her in a shop, a white mum –

MARY – It's always a white mum –

LYSANDER – will lean down and ask him:

WHITE MUM Oh, darling where's your mummy?

LYSANDER But right now, back on the street, Mary is very concerned about their apparent difference because they have caught the eye of a passing police officer.

MARY A young police officer, who's white.

LYSANDER He watches them, intrigued. At least I think it's intrigue. We won't spend enough time with this character to really know what makes him tick.

MARY But he's a police officer in the eighties so it's probably a cocktail of cocaine, hatred and Phil Collins.

We hear a Phil Collins drum solo.

LYSANDER So, he watches them.

MARY Mary pulls the boy a little less hard. The boy does not return the favour.

LYSANDER The officer crosses the road towards them.

MARY Mary keeps moving. Not sure if she should just stop or if that will make them look more suspicious.

LYSANDER The boy continues to tug. Tug. Tug. Tug...

MARY Enough!

She turns on **LYSANDER**.

The officer is moving faster towards them. Mary tries to pull the boy along quicker now...

LYSANDER But then the boy spots the police officer and... BING! It hits him. He knows exactly what to do:

BOY Mummy if you don't buy that toy for me, I'll tell the policeman you've kidnapped me.

MARY What did you say?!

BOY I'll tell that policeman that /you

MARY /For a second Mary can't help but laugh at how sophisticated this diabolical statement is –

LYSANDER – The officer is two feet away. Nearly upon them.

MARY Please Lysander...

LYSANDER Yes, that is his name. She has named him Lysander. What can I say? She's an artist.

MARY Or at least she aspires to be.

Back to the scene.

Ok. Fine. You win.

LYSANDER So, I can definitely have/the

MARY /Yes! You can have the toy just /stop

LYSANDER /The policeman is beside them. But before he can utter a word –

– We hear a radio crackle.

POLICE RADIO All units to Hanover Street. I repeat all units to Hanover Street, we have an assault and battery.

LYSANDER The officer says something into his radio, stares at our odd couple one last time then spins on his heel and walks off in the other direction.

She turns to sharply to **LYSANDER.**

MARY You little shit! How did you... Where did that come from?

LYSANDER Can we go back and get the toy then?

MARY Fuck me... You are my son Lysander. There are a lot of people who won't believe it, but you must always say that you are my son.

LYSANDER Lysander finally sees the sincerity, the pain in her eyes and immediately feels guilty. It is hard to know if he was fully aware of what he meant by the statement. If he was aware of the racial implications and the danger he was putting his mother in –

MARY – But it's also hard to argue that he wasn't.

#2

We see the logo of a company called Four Walls projected on the back wall. **LYSANDER** *is stood in front of it.* **MARY** *sits in the audience.*

LYSANDER Hello? Right... Well first off thank you all for coming along today. It's so nice to see some familiar faces too! Now for those of you who don't know me I'm Lysander and I am liaison and adviser here at Four Walls. But I also grew up in this estate. Block A, Flat 18. Without somewhere like Culross me and my mother would have been on the streets. I've spent my whole life fighting for social housing in London, and before we start let me address the elephant in the room. I know you are all feeling pretty suspicious right now, but I can assure you we're not here to knock down your flats or move any of you out –

LILLY – This is a joke right?

LYSANDER Lilly?

LILLY Hello Lysander.

LYSANDER Nice to see you.

LILLY Yeah. Seriously is this a joke? You work for a housing company?

LYSANDER It's not like that. I'm here to help Culross.

LILLY By knocking it down?

LYSANDER That's the opposite of what we're doing here. Look /I

LILLY /I mean this whole thing is setting off some serious fucking alarm bells.

LYSANDER *turns to us.*

LYSANDER So this is Lilly.

LILLY *becomes* **MARY** *again.*

MARY She lived on Culross with us.

LYSANDER She was two years younger than me.

MARY A sweet kid.

LYSANDER I found her annoying to be honest and we haven't seen each other in about twenty years. Have some mutual friends on Facebook though.

MARY *becomes* LILLY *again.*

Lilly I get what you think this is, but this isn't that. If you just let me speak. Please?

LILLY Speak.

LYSANDER Thank you.

LILLY My pleasure.

Beat.

LYSANDER Ok. Look we all know that social housing is being made extinct right? The government has cut spending and the council is under insane pressure to build new homes as well as refurbish old ones following what happened at Grenfell, and there are a lot of people, including housing associations, taking advantage of this. But Four Walls are here to stop all that. We bridge the gap between housing associations, councils and tenants to come up with ways to keep social housing safe whilst providing enough new homes and funding to keep the council happy.

LILLY So how do you build more flats without knocking down ours?

LYSANDER We look at non-invasive options. We find areas around the estate or build on the existing structure.

LILLY Oh, so you turn the estate into a building site?

Beat.

LYSANDER We haven't looked at all the options yet. This meeting is a discussion so we can find out what best suits everyone.

LILLY Well I can answer that for you. We'd just like some repairs done to the current flats and the housing association to stop sending useless cowboys whenever we need something fixed. That's it, thanks. Meeting adjourned?

LYSANDER Look we want that too but... I'm trying to be as honest with you as possible here. We need to build some private flats to pay for the upkeep and repairs of Culross. That's the only way to fund any of this. We have to find a compromise.

LILLY *laughs.*

LILLY For you lot it's a compromise but for us it's an ultimatum.

LYSANDER We're trying to /help

LILLY /Do you really believe the words coming out of your mouth right now? I mean... You know... You know the minute we let any "redevelopment" near this estate it... It will be like opening a window on the Titanic. All the assholes will come flooding in and they'll strip the place for everything. We're the last place standing in this shiny glass sea of shit and... that's because we fight. You know that, yet you're trying to convince us to negotiate with the fucking iceberg.

LYSANDER No! I'm trying to make sure that when the iceberg hits it doesn't sink... This analogy doesn't work. I knew the vultures were circling Culross and that's the reason I suggested it to Four Walls, so we could save it. I promise you nobody is losing their home here. This was my home too.

Silence.

LILLY What would your mum think about this then?

#3

We see an image of a large block of flats outside King's Cross station in the eighties. This is Culross. **MARY** *and* **LYSANDER** *go to opposite sides of the stage.*

MARY It was originally built for builders. For the builders who were building the station. Laying the tracks. The guys you see grinning in those black and white photos, covered in dirt, looking fulfilled.

We see a photo of those guys grinning.

Looking like they were making a difference. They slept six to a flat. Dreaming of the future. Of the millions of people that would be using the wonderful building they had built. Once the station was finished and builders moved on to their next world-changing endeavour, the flats were filled with families. Crammed high with them.

LYSANDER Then as time went on, they became more rundown, dangerous. The prostitutes and drug dealers moved in and slowly but surely King's Cross became the boil on London's back...

We see prostitutes, drug dealers and images of a rundown King's Cross.

And Culross Buildings was its pusy head.

We now see Culross Buildings.

MARY I moved in straight after I fell pregnant with Lysander. When I was nineteen and had to drop out of art school. Nothing like a child to destroy your dreams.

LYSANDER *gives her a look and she shrugs.*

LYSANDER Art school is where she met my dad.

MARY He did a runner before Lysander was born.

LYSANDER But luckily the government was kinder to single mothers back then.

MARY Like a serial killer is kinder to its neighbour so as not to raise suspicions. I'd never had my own place before. And hadn't felt welcome in my mum's house for a while. So even though it was what some people might call a cesspit –

LYSANDER – It was a cesspit –

MARY – We called it –

BOTH – home.

MARY The prostitutes could be fairly pleasant, and the drug dealers had other things to worry about than us.

LYSANDER The only gang on the estate would always leave me alone because:

GANG MEMBER Leave him. His mum's black.

LYSANDER I'd got used to my mother shooing me away from the window whenever there was an unlawful sex act taking place. Or the monthly swat raids on the drugs den at the end of the block.

MARY And the flats were actually really well built. High ceilings and large windows. So, it started to attract other young families with no cash who wanted to build a life in the big city. Sayed and his mother Adhira moved down from Liverpool. She'd run away from an arranged marriage in India and raised Sayed on her own in England.

We see a photo of Sayed and Adhira.

LYSANDER I liked them.

MARY Then there was Emma and her husband Jack.

LYSANDER Emma and mum didn't see eye-to-eye.

We now see Emma and Jack.

MARY Because she was a racist fucking bitch. And then there was Lilly and her parents Adowa and Jane. Jane's parents had disowned her for marrying a black man.

We see a photo of young **LILLY** *with Adowa and Jane.*

LYSANDER Back then you couldn't have a mixed-race relationship without a bit of disownment.

MARY And then there were the young penniless artists trying to make it big in the big city. Graham in flat sixteen was from Scotland and wanted to be a novelist.

GRAHAM It's going to be like Trainspotting but set in Kentish Town.

LYSANDER Milly and Nick were poshos who were slumming it because they really wanted to be gritty movie directors.

NICK We want to capture the real heart of this city. Show the unfair disparities between the rich and poor...

MARY And Jason just above was a chef from South London.

JASON I wanna create no nonsense cooking for geezers on the go, you know what I mean. I'll put my own spin on the bacon butty. Pukka mate.

MARY And I'm a...painter. Who's never been paid for a piece of work.

LYSANDER So, she had to find any jobs she could to keep us afloat.

MARY Which was tricky when a lot of places didn't want to employ a black woman.

We now see cranes and building sites.

LYSANDER The shadow of demolition always hung over Culross. From the day we moved in. There where huge plans to build the Channel Tunnel and "regenerate" the area. It wasn't clear how far reaching this was going to be but Culross had been marked for death.

MARY But we fought. We fought the council every day to keep it standing.

LYSANDER And knowing your home could be taken at any minute made Mary want one thing more than anything –

MARY – To paint. *(Beat)* And be paid for it.

#4

We now see a large painting of a handsome, bald black man in his early thirties.

MARY *is stood beside it looking very nervous. A* **GALLERIST** *examines it.*

GALLERIST Interesting. Very interesting. Explain it to me.

MARY Explain it?

GALLERIST Tell me what it means?

MARY Ok. Well... Well it's my dad.

GALLERIST Right. Ok. But what is it...saying?

MARY It's a portrait.

GALLERIST I can see that but what are you saying with it?

MARY Here's a portrait of my dad?

GALLERIST Right...

The **GALLERIST** *doesn't look impressed.* **MARY** *turns to us.*

MARY We've all met this guy at some point, right? Fuck some of you probably are him. He's called Humphrey or Lucien or Hugo –

GALLERIST – Gillian.

MARY Gillian. Fuck me. He's white. Born into money and skipped straight from Eton or Harrow to gap year to Oxford.

GALLERIST Oxford Brookes actually.

***MARY** looks at him a little shocked.*

Yeah. It was tough.

MARY And sure, he knows he's had a "slight" helping hand, but he's also worked really hard to get to where he is today.

GALLERIST Thank you.

MARY Yes, it's because of his sophisticated artistic taste that he runs this place and nothing to do with his dad's best friend owning this gallery.

GALLERIST What can I say? He saw something in me.

MARY Yeah. Himself. *(Beat)* I've been rejected by nearly every gallery in London, but Gillian has a strong interest in –

GALLERIST – Silenced voices.

MARY So he's taken an interest in mine.

Back to him.

MARY Ok... I haven't seen my dad for a long time... Since I was a kid. He's in Jamaica... So I guess painting him... I guess it's me connecting with /him

GALLERIST /Can I give you some advice?

MARY Yeah.

GALLERIST Anyone can paint a portrait.

MARY Ok.

GALLERIST Your strength lies in your blackness.

Beat.

MARY My blackness?

GALLERIST Yes! Weaponise it.

MARY Weaponise my blackness?

GALLERIST Your people are out there rioting in the streets no? What is the black experience in this city right now? Show me that? Bring me something controversial! Something with edge! Something that will make the art world think... now this is a voice.

MARY Um... Right.

GALLERIST Bring me something like that and we're in business.

Pause.

MARY Right. So, you want me to go away and paint a new painting?

GALLERIST You'll need a few if you want to put an exhibition on?

MARY That will take me months.

GALLERIST Don't rush it.

MARY Right.

GALLERIST I can't wait to see what you come up with.

MARY Neither can I.

We now see an architect's plan for a block of flats projected onto the wall.

LYSANDER *goes and stands in front of it.* **HARRIET** *examines it.*

HARRIET Interesting... So, we don't make any changes to the estate at all?

LYSANDER Exactly. We build a new block of private flats in the space between the flats and the carpark and use the money from those to fund the refurb of Culross at no extra cost to the council.

HARRIET So how many new flats will we be building?

LYSANDER Six.

HARRIET Six?

LYSANDER I know it doesn't sound like many but if we sell them at a high enough price then it should be enough to maintain the upkeep of Culross. The building itself is structurally sound.

Beat.

HARRIET This is fantastic.

LYSANDER Thank you.

HARRIET Seriously Lysander I'm really proud of you.

LYSANDER Um... Thank you.

HARRIET You should be proud of yourself.

LYSANDER Yes. So you think we could propose this then?

HARRIET No.

LYSANDER *turns to us.*

LYSANDER This is my boss Harriet.

HARRIET Harry.

LYSANDER Harry. She's white and northern and has worked her way up from nothing to start Four Walls. She's always saying things like:

HARRIET We have to help the helpless.

LYSANDER Or:

HARRIET We shout for those without a voice.

LYSANDER She did work in the city as a trader for a few years –

HARRIET – It was fucking disgusting –

LYSANDER – But she made some money then decided to give something back.

HARRIET I grew up in a council flat and I saw what this government was doing to them so I started this company. And every year the money gets less, the requirements get harder and the press gets worse. But we are making a difference.

LYSANDER I was working for a homeless charity when I met her and I was struggling to make any difference and...well she seemed to be making some sense.

HARRIET We work the system from the inside. This is a capitalist country so we have to make capitalism work for us.

LYSANDER Plus I really need a proper pay check as I have a baby on the way.

HARRIET How far along?

LYSANDER Five months.

HARRIET Congratulations.

Back to the scene.

LYSANDER But I think this is a strong option.

HARRIET That's why I hired you. So much passion. But we need to explore the complete refurbishment options.

LYSANDER But I thought that was only if we couldn't –

HARRIET – Build enough flats. And six isn't enough flats. Look you've always known this was on the table Lysander. We knock it down. Rebuild it bigger and better than before and make sure it's majority social housing. Any other company would try and make a packet off this estate (I mean you could make a mint). And six flats means we're not even covering our costs.

LYSANDER Yes but... The building is structurally sound and I just think... Let me see if there's any other options.

Beat.

HARRIET Of course, but... Is this about that black woman at the meeting?

LYSANDER Lilly?

HARRIET She seemed pretty angry.

LYSANDER Um... I wouldn't say /that

HARRIET /You know her?

LYSANDER Yeah, she lived on the estate when we were kids.

HARRIET Right. Black women can be...tricky. *(Beat)* It's ok my husband's black.

LYSANDER My mum's actually...

HARRIET What?

LYSANDER Nothing.

HARRIET Is Lilly going to be a problem?

LYSANDER I don't think so.

HARRIET Good. And look, I know this is personal to you, but don't forget we need to make some profit here too. The more we build the more lucrative this is for us and the more we can invest in other estates in the future.

LYSANDER Of course but... Let me just speak to the architects again.

Pause.

HARRIET Ok. I can't wait to see what you come up with.

#6

MARY and LYSANDER stand on either side of the stage. Lysander is looking at building plans whilst Mary tries to paint.

MARY I've been trying to paint but nothing's coming –

LYSANDER – I can't stare at building plans any longer –

MARY – I'm so uninspired –

LYSANDER – I need to clear my mind –

MARY – Let off some steam –

LYSANDER – There's only one solution:

BOTH DRUGS!

We see pill'd up ravers gurning to house music. **MARY** *starts getting ready for a night out.*

MARY Pills! Ecstasy. Beans. Uppers. The drug of choice for every twenty something kicking out at the weekend in the early nineties. Take two or three and see you in the morning. Madforit. When it comes to Friday night everyone is on them. Weed is too chill, Acid too... Acid, and cocaine...well that's too fucking expensive. That's the city cunts drug of choice. Pills are the high of the people. I took my first one at fifteen and my god... I had the time of my life. Turns out I was just staring at a disco ball all night...but it was a fucking beautiful disco ball. But then Lysander came along and...no more fun... Well tonight that's going to change.

LYSANDER *is waiting for a drug dealer to turn up. He keeps looking at his phone.*

LYSANDER I saw this funny tweet once that said the two things you learn when you grow up are: nobody really cares about you, and EVERYBODY does cocaine. On a Friday night in London there isn't a toilet seat that hasn't got a line being done on it. From the grotty pubs to high-end restaurants, you'll always find two to a cubicle and lot of chat. House parties on council estates or dinner parties on grand estates, rich and poor, old and young, good and bad everyone enjoys a line on a Friday night. I fall into the category of the weekend addict. Monday to Thurs we're fine (well maybe there's a little wobble on a Thurs if it's a sunny day) but come Friday night without fail. It's line time. I never go out without a gram in my pocket. One gram if I'm seeing friends. Two for my girlfriend's friends and three for family. *(Beat)* Only joking. Six grams for family.

MARY My old school friend Noah has invited me out. I haven't really seen him since I moved to Culross, but I bumped into him at the supermarket and he told me a bunch of the old gang were heading out to a warehouse party. Maybe a night out will get those creative juices flowing again. So, I left Lysander with Jason the chef and got dressed to the nines (maybe more a seven). The party is in a warehouse in Peckham. It would have to be fucking Peckham. I fucking hate South.

LYSANDER I'm currently on route to my girlfriend's private view in a private members club in Peckham. Crossing the river in an Uber. I never go South but this is my girlfriend's first big show and...and well I haven't got a choice really.

Now we see nineties Peckham. Still busy but more edgy.

MARY We got off the bus about twenty minutes ago and we're fucking lost. But my half has kicked in so walking around Peckham is far less scary with a head full of serotonin. It's actually not as intimidating as I thought. It just feels a bit... forgotten. Rundown shops and broken street lights.

We see modern Peckham. All gentrified and busy.

LYSANDER Peckham's lovely actually. Nicer than I remember. The streets are packed with trendy media types getting pissed at pop up bars or stumbling out of gastro pubs.

MARY Then we pass a pub where there's a group of old men outside and one of them shouts:

PUB MAN Why don't you go back to where you fucking came from!

Pause.

MARY It hangs in the air for a second. Now Noah and the rest of my gang are white and they're not sure how to handle this situation, but sadly this is not the first time I've had something like this shouted at me and it definitely won't be the last. I refuse to let this cunt ruin my night though, so I give him an aggressive smile and say: What? Watford?

We see the exterior of a warehouse.

LYSANDER I finally arrive at the members bar. It's in a renovated old –

MARY – Warehouse. It looks dodgy as fuck. A big nondescript grey building with huge metal doors –

We start to hear some sort of chillout Dub music.

LYSANDER – Inside is...fancy. They've done a decent job of it. Dark woods and exposed stone walls. Nice furniture. Prob same interior designers as the Soho House people. Toilets have all the perfect surfaces. Because private members bars are essentially the brown paper bags of the cocaine industry. Every member does it care free and easy without any trouble from the law. There are a lot of people here. Even the odd celebrity. New money and old.

Back to **MARY**. *Her party is playing loud Jungle music.*

MARY This place is pretty rundown but it's pumping. A real eclectic mix of people. Young, old. Punks, Goths and drag queens. Black, white and everything in between. Think Studio 54 if Studio 54 was a dirty fucking rave in South London. I take another half and head over to the makeshift bar.

Back to **LYSANDER.**

LYSANDER I look around for Ruby.

Back to **MARY.**

MARY There's a tall handsome black guy standing by the makeshift bar. Now I've only ever dated white guys but... He smiles at me.

MARY *smiles back.*

Ok.

Back to **LYSANDER.**

LYSANDER And there she is. The current love of my life. Ruby Robinson-Lane. She's middle class. And white. And she's just starting to show. Fuck I can't believe we're having a fucking baby! I met her about four years ago at a pub in Camden and we immediately hit it off. She's a photographer slash stylist slash writer slash stunning. And tonight's her first big exhibition. Entitled: "The city with a thousand faces".

We see **RUBY***'s photos. Different types of people throughout London. Different ethnicities, age, size and gender.*

Back to **MARY.**

MARY The black guy grabs his beer and walk over to me. He's wearing a red polo neck jumper and looks like he could be...a poet or a...sexy school teacher.

DARREN Hey?

MARY Hey?

DARREN I'm Darren.

MARY I'm Darren... I mean I'm Mary. *(To us)* Fuck!

Back to **LYSANDER.**

LYSANDER Ruby is chatting to some old white guy, maybe a journalist or something. She rests her hand on her stomach. I feel a bit sick.

RUBY *goes over to him.*

RUBY Hello darling?

LYSANDER Hey babe. This is amazing. What a turn out!

RUBY I know we might even get featured in the Standard tomorrow.

LYSANDER Exciting!

RUBY I know.

LYSANDER How you feeling?

RUBY Good. It's been a bit hectic, but I can relax now.

LYSANDER Good.

RUBY I've got a bit of bad news though...

Back to MARY.

MARY So, what do you do Darren?

DARREN I teach poetry.

MARY No way! Amazing.

DARREN You?

MARY I'm an artist.

DARREN What type of stuff?

MARY Portraits, I guess.

DARREN Cool.

MARY I'm struggling at the moment though.

Back to LYSANDER.

LYSANDER What bad news?

RUBY Our offer on that flat fell through.

LYSANDER Fuck!

RUBY Someone put in a higher bid.

LYSANDER Fuck's sake! I thought that was ours. It took us months to find that.

RUBY I know.

LYSANDER How high?

RUBY Out of our price range.

LYSANDER FUCK!

Back to **MARY**.

MARY The curator (or whatever you call them) of this gallery wants to me to paint the...black experience or something...

DARREN *(laughing)* Of course.

MARY And... I don't know what that means. My experience is... One-minute people are asking if my son is mine and the next they're telling me to go home. All my friends are white, and I don't really speak to my family and... Sorry I'm a bit high.

DARREN You have a son?

MARY Fuck. Maybe should have held back on that fact for a bit longer.

Back to **LYSANDER**.

LYSANDER But we have to be out of our place by the end of the month. We're not going to be able to find somewhere else before then. Fuck!

RUBY I asked my parents, but they've already leant us so much –

LYSANDER – Fuck, fuck, fuck.

RUBY It's fine darling we'll just have to keep looking.

LYSANDER No, it's not fine.

Back to **MARY.**

MARY Yeah, I have a son. And he's white. *(To us)* Fuck it. My drugs have kicked in now so there's no stopping this. *(Back to* **DARREN***)* And I hate him. No. I don't actually hate him but... I hate how he makes me feel. When he was born, he was so white. His dad's from Manchester...but I... I just wasn't prepared for...

Back to **LYSANDER.**

LYSANDER That place was the cheapest we could find, and it was still out of our price range! We need to find somewhere... Jesus... We can't be sleeping on some mate's sofa with a baby on the way.

Back to **MARY.**

MARY He was so fucking white and... I thought having a child would finally make me feel connected to something...

Back to **LYSANDER.**

LYSANDER We're gonna have to find more money. We have to top that offer!

MARY My whole life I've felt so outside from everything... detached...and I thought having him would change that... but it's just made me feel even more...alone.

DARREN Well...you should paint that then.

Pause.

LYSANDER I need another line... I leave Ruby and find the closest toilet.

MARY Fuck Darren is hot. I grab him and pull him over to the wall and we start making out.

LYSANDER I do the fattest line possible. YESSS! I don't want to think... I just... I head through to the dance floor in another room. Well I say dance floor but it's basically just some coked up media types shuffling from foot to foot.

We start to hear "OUT OF SPACE" by The Prodigy.*

MARY We're going for it but then this song comes on –

LYSANDER – Fuck. I haven't heard this in ages –

MARY – I've never heard it before but –

LYSANDER – What a tune!

MARY It's like break beat mixed with an old reggae tune and it's –

LYSANDER – Fucking awesome.

MARY I want to dance –

LYSANDER – I'm on the dance floor –

MARY – and I'm engulfed by the sweat and music...

They both start dancing to song.

MARY AND LYSANDER What a classic!

They both dance. Losing themselves in the music. Trying to forget but then they see each other.

MARY And then I see him –

LYSANDER – I see my mother –

MARY – Lysander –

LYSANDER – And I see her pain –

MARY – It suddenly becomes clear to me –

LYSANDER – I can't let what happened to her happen to me –

MARY – I know exactly what I should paint...

#7

We now see an image of **MARY** *with a white baby in her arms. Only it's a reworking of the famous Madonna with child image.*

MARY *stands beside it proudly. The* **GALLERIST** *looks uncomfortable.*

MARY What do you think?

GALLERIST I... Um...

MARY Do you want me to explain it?

GALLERIST Well...

MARY It's a self-portrait... A play on the classic image of Madonna and child. Which is ironic really.

GALLERIST Why?

MARY Because my name's Mary. After the Tina Turner song though.

GALLERIST No why have you painted this?

MARY Oh because I'm a mother. And my son is white, and I feel like... Well I don't feel like a great mother to him... So I painted myself as this perfect /idea

GALLERIST /No this isn't right.

Pause.

MARY But you asked me for my black experience and... /well

GALLERIST /I was expecting something more visceral. Like black people rioting or...police brutality or something...but this... I don't know what this is.

MARY I just told you.

GALLERIST I'm sorry but... No this won't work...

MARY Why?

GALLERIST Because it's not what I wanted. Paint me something else.

MARY What...?

GALLERIST This isn't right Mary.

MARY Right...

Pause.

I'm sorry... But you say you like my "voice" correct?

GALLERIST It has potential.

MARY Ok. And you know I have a son? And making enough money to support us both...is hard. Fucking hard. And trying to find time to paint well... I'm sure you can imagine it's very tricky finding the time to do fucking anything. Especially as I'm making no money from it and now you... You want me to go away and start /again

GALLERIST /I'm sorry but there's no /other

MARY /I'm sure the never-ending stream of middle-class artists that you usually deal with can afford to just take another loan off mummy and daddy and go and do that but...but voices like mine...voices that you say there aren't enough of, we can't do that. Because every time we create a piece of work it costs us everything... And then we are at the whim of people like you...people on nice little wages, who go on lovely little holidays and have delightful little dinner parties where they talk about the wonderful talent they've just discovered. Who then want to warp that talent into something that suits their fucking... "tastes". That can be digested at those delicate little dinner parties. And that's only if that talent hasn't starved to death trying to please you first.

GALLERIST Look... This is a business. A business like any other. We need to cater to the customer. Contrary to popular belief that is how the art world has always worked. And yes, my customers are white wealthy people. And I understand exactly what they want. What they desire. And yes, you might have to compromise for it. You'll have to work for it. Because that's what separates the paid artist from the broke ones.

MARY *sighs.*

MARY I don't have time to fucking compromise.

LYSANDER *stands in front of a new set of building plans.*
HARRIET *sits in front of him.*

LYSANDER Harriet?

HARRIET What have I told you?

LYSANDER Harry.

HARRIET So, these are your new plans?

LYSANDER Yeah... Um... So, after some deliberation, I think...
I think you were probably right.

HARRIET It wouldn't be the first time.

LYSANDER Complete refurbishment might be the only way to
deliver what the council wants, create more social housing
and guarantee the current residents can return.

HARRIET I knew you'd get there in the end.

LYSANDER Yes...

HARRIET So how many private flats are we building?

LYSANDER Well... With this new building design... There will
be about a hundred flats in total so I was thinking about
twenty private ones would be enough to fund the project
and make the company some money.

Beat.

HARRIET This is great Lysander. Really great. I know it must
be tough for you, knocking down your old home but... This
is the right way to do it.

LYSANDER Yes...and I...erm... I was wondering... In terms of...
You said this would be lucrative to the company, right?

HARRIET Yes.

LYSANDER Well... As I suggested Culross... I was wondering...

HARRIET Ha! Of course. I said this would be lucrative for all
of us.

LYSANDER Great.

HARRIET But you know... This has got me thinking. We have an opportunity here. The council are very keen to build a lot of homes and I'm thinking... Well if we make sixty percent of the flats private than we could make a lot more money to help fund our future projects.

LYSANDER Sixty? But that's...way above what... We've promised everyone can return /and

HARRIET /I know! I know and we'll still make that happen. But... Do you know how many people actually return after they have to upheave their whole life to somewhere for two or three years? Zero. Maybe one.

LYSANDER Yeah but I don't think we /should

HARRIET /This is an opportunity to increase our funds Lysander. So, we can help more projects in the future.

LYSANDER No, I don't think /that's

HARRIET And of course, that would make it even more lucrative for us... The company.

LYSANDER I don't think we should... That's too many...

HARRIET I don't think you understand me. This is the only way Lysander and if this is too hard for you then maybe you shouldn't be overseeing this project at all.

Silence. He doesn't say anything.

Also, your old friend... That black woman from the meeting.

LYSANDER Lilly?

HARRIET Yes. She's kicking up quite a fuss. National paper fuss. And that will make it harder for the council to approve our plans so... Go and speak to her. Get her on side.

LYSANDER She won't listen to me.

HARRIET You have history, right? Use it.

We see a boat on the ocean.

MARY Thirty days at sea. Thirty days of dreaming.

LYSANDER Twenty-eight pounds a ticket.

MARY A thousand pounds today.

LYSANDER The boat was filled with music.

MARY If you have more than three Jamaicans together, you've got yourself a party.

LYSANDER And if there's one thing that grandad loved –

MARY It was a party.

We see London in the 1950s.

LYSANDER He arrived in England in the 1950s and the first things he noticed was:

GRANDAD The cold weather.

LYSANDER Why don't you go back to where you came from!

GRANDAD And the warm welcome.

LYSANDER But he had a plan.

GRANDAD I work hard for five years than go back home a wealthy man.

LYSANDER And he got a job in construction.

GRANDAD Rebuild England brick by brick.

LYSANDER At first, he hated London but then one thing changed that:

*We now see **MARY**'s mother.*

MARY My mother was a shop girl from Scotland and was sharing a room with her best friend Irene.

GRANDMA She snored like a bloody horse.

MARY She moved to London with the dream of opening her own clothes shop.

GRANDMA I'll save every penny I have.

MARY Which was tricky as she spent every penny on going out.

GRANDMA You gotta have some fun sometimes too.

MARY And then one night her and Irene found themselves in a basement club in Clapham. Jamaicans had found that the best way of getting around the racism of white clubs was to make their own.

We hear some ska music and GRANDMA *and* GRANDAD *go to opposite sides of the stage.*

LYSANDER Grandma hadn't been around this many black people before, but she was trying to play it cool.

We see GRANDMA *playing it cool.*

MARY As soon as dad walked in, she caught his eye.

LYSANDER Grandma said she didn't like the look of him at first. Too arrogant.

MARY But then dad tried to win her over with his moves.

The Ska tunes builds and GRANDAD *dances over to* GRANDMA.

LYSANDER Grandma says she rejected him at first –

She rejects him.

MARY – But dad persevered.

GRANDAD *dances near her again and makes her laugh. She gives in and they dance together...*

LYSANDER They became a couple pretty soon after that.

MARY And pretty soon after that mum got pregnant with me.

GRANDMA Nothing like a child to ruin your dreams.

MARY *smiles.*

MARY And suck away your savings.

LYSANDER They couldn't afford a house in London.

MARY So, dad thought they'd have better luck in Jamaica so they packed their bags and left.

LYSANDER Thirty days at sea. Thirty days of dreaming.

MARY They arrived in Jamaica in the 60's and the first thing mum noticed was the:

GRANDMA Hot weather.

JAMAICAN WOMAN What's a white woman doing in Kingston?

GRANDMA And the cold stares.

MARY They bought a house –

LYSANDER – But Jamaica was tough.

MARY At school I was bullied for being British.

LYSANDER Grandma was worried about her daughter –

MARY – And her and dad argued a lot.

LYSANDER In the end Grandma decided it would be better for mum in England so they left Grandad behind.

MARY Thirty days at sea. Thirty days of crying.

LYSANDER It broke grandma's heart.

MARY The things we do for love.

The ska song plays again but then in fades into **"I DON'T CARE"** *by Ed Sheeran & Justin Bieber.**

---

* A licence to produce WHITEWASH does not include a performance licence for "I DON'T CARE". For further information, please see Music Use Note on page v.

#10

LYSANDER and RUBY now dance together. LYSANDER is distracted. RUBY is loving it.

RUBY What is this song?

LYSANDER I think it's Justin Bieber.

RUBY I love it.

LYSANDER Yes it's not bad. Can we get some air?

RUBY Oh... Ok.

They head outside. RUBY sits.

LYSANDER Do you want anything?

RUBY No, I'm fine.

He sits down next to her.

Such a beautiful venue, isn't it?

LYSANDER Yeah. *(beat)* Must have cost them a packet.

RUBY You can't put a price on a day like this.

LYSANDER I bet they did.

RUBY smiles.

RUBY Well it's still lovely.

LYSANDER Yeah.

Silence.

I'm sorry. I know we should be doing this but –

RUBY – It's ok. We're in no rush.

LYSANDER Yeah but... I'm sorry.

Pause.

RUBY What's wrong with you at the moment?

LYSANDER Nothing I just... It's my job.

RUBY What about it?

LYSANDER I just... I don't know Ruby... I don't think I should be doing it.

Pause.

RUBY What?!

LYSANDER They want me to sell off my old home and... I can't.

RUBY You can't?

LYSANDER No.

RUBY Don't do this. Not now. Are you joking?

LYSANDER No, I –

RUBY – I can't listen to this. Are you seriously saying this right now? We have to go and stay at my parents' house and we have a baby on the way and... Jesus I've tried to be positive about this but... The whole reason you took this job was because your charity work (which I completely supported by the way) wasn't paying enough and now... You've been acting so strange recently and... I can't even tell you how I'm really feeling...

She's trying to stop herself from crying.

LYSANDER I'm sorry.

RUBY I'm scared, Lysander.

LYSANDER No... No don't be scared... Just forget I said anything I was just... It's gonna be fine. I'll sort it.

RUBY Really?

LYSANDER Yes. Really.

Beat.

I love you.

RUBY I love you too.

Reggae music plays.

MARY One of the main things that surprises me about Jamaica is that for such a homophobic country it is incredibly camp. We're currently at a street party in downtown Kingston.

We see images of a street party in Jamaica.

LYSANDER Now when she says street party, she means street party. A spontaneous party in the street. This is nothing like Notting Hill Carnival. No fenced off areas, portaloos or gangs of posh white kids here.

We see images of Notting Hill Carnival.

MARY A huge sound system has been pulled into the middle of a quiet residential road and Jamaicans of all ages are letting loose. Literally all ages.

LYSANDER Old ladies (in what look like their wedding dresses) dancing with muscly topless eighteen-year olds. Scantily clad women grind with brightly shirted old men. Rastafarians sway to the beat, and there are a lot of Asian Jamaicans going for it too.

MARY The festivities are constantly interrupted by cars trying to get down the street.

LYSANDER And each time the party splits like the hockey game in Wayne's World.

WAYNE CAR!

MARY Then reconnects like nothing has happened.

LYSANDER I'm fourteen and my face is the only white one here. I say white but it's actually sunburnt red now. Since me and mum arrived two days ago, I've desperately tried to get a tan. To fit in.

MARY Feeling out of place because of skin colour is usually my specialist subject. But that's not my problem here. In fact, people think I'm one of the wealthy uptown Jamaicans. It's strange.

LYSANDER This country is like the purest expression of human desire. Sex and partying followed by guilt and religion. Next to every bar there is a church.

MARY Jamaicans don't hide their feelings, they wear them with pride.

LYSANDER What looks like a violent blazing row is just a passionate discussion. Apparently.

MARY I had forgotten this, but it hasn't taken long for me to start relishing it. Some long-buried part of me has started to rise to the surface

LYSANDER And she's quickly becoming as confrontational as the best of them.

MARY No, I'm not.

They both smile.

LYSANDER Ever since we got here mum's had a smile on her face. I've not seen her smile this much in a long time. Back in London, Culross is still under threat and money is just as scarce.

MARY And then my mother died.

We see a photo of MARY *with her mother.*

Cancer.

LYSANDER So, mum needed to get away.

MARY What little inheritance there was I used on two plane tickets.

LYSANDER I would have preferred a PlayStation.

MARY I wanted to revisit my Jamaican heritage. And see my father again.

LYSANDER Nobody believes me and granddad are related. Everything about us is opposite. A short, bald, black man with a thick Jamaican accent and a tall, white, skinny teenager with an over-pronounced British one.

MARY My father has a short temper and unbridled energy. At sixty-five he still drinks and parties like he's forty years younger.

GRANDAD You're not old till you think you're old.

MARY After my mother he got married two more times but never divorced (you do the maths) and was shot once. By a hitman hired by his second wife who was protesting the third. He was handsome when he was younger and retains a lot of that charm in his twilight years. Cutting quite a figure in a white fedora and large selection of brightly coloured silk shirts.

GRANDAD Handmade in Cuba.

MARY He often claimed loudly to those who asked.

LYSANDER And those who didn't.

MARY I guess.... I just want to try and connect with him. And find out why he never came over to see me after we left.

LYSANDER But even though we've spent all our time with him since we arrived here, mum and her father haven't really talked.

MARY For a sixty-five-year-old man he really does have a hectic life. He's driven us to three dominoes games –

LYSANDER – Where we had to sit at the back of the room in silence.

MARY Two women's houses –

LYSANDER – Where we had to sit outside in the car in silence.

MARY And one mobile phone shop –

LYSANDER – Where he tried to convince us to buy him a new mobile phone.

MARY And this was only the first day. Needless to say, there was no time for actual conversation.

LYSANDER – And when the same schedule happened on the second day mum wondered if this was all on purpose. If he just didn't really want to speak with her.

MARY So, I'm hoping that, in the more relaxed air of the street party, I can finally talk to my father.

LYSANDER – They went off together about ten minutes ago and left my bright red face standing here by the bar. A young Jamaican woman, in a neon green dress, has cornered me and is asking me questions about my home country. I find all the women here intimidating –

MARY – I find all the women here powerful. I'm starting to believe that it is in fact the women who run Jamaica and not the men. They don't fuck about. I wonder if England has killed this power in me… or if it was just never there in the first place.

JAMAICAN WOMAN I'd love to go to England you know.

LYSANDER – Erm… You should. It's nice.

JAMAICAN WOMAN Maybe a nice rich boy like you take me?

LYSANDER – Erm… I'm afraid I'm not rich.

JAMAICAN WOMAN You fly here didn't you?

LYSANDER – Yes but /I didn't

JAMAICAN WOMAN /You afford a plane ticket then you rich.

LYSANDER – Um... I'm really not. Then I spot a white fedora in the distance.

Back to woman.

LYSANDER Sorry I've got to go.

JAMAICAN WOMAN You come right back, baby boy!

LYSANDER The only light on the party comes from house windows so there are huge pockets of darkness. As I move further from the bar, I start to become more and more unsettled. I push past people and they stare at me suspiciously. Then I accidently knock into a huge guy in a bright shirt.

JAMAICAN MAN Watch where you going white boy.

LYSANDER Sorry I...

JAMAICAN MAN You a fed?

LYSANDER No.

JAMAICAN MAN Where you from? Australia?

LYSANDER England.

JAMAICAN MAN I hate the English. Love the Irish but me hate the English.

LYSANDER Um... Ok.

JAMAICAN MAN The Irish bomb the English.

LYSANDER Yes. Yes they did.

JAMAICAN MAN What you doing here?

LYSANDER I'm visiting my granddad. He's from here... From Kingston... He's black!

Beat.

JAMAICAN MAN What you say?

LYSANDER He's black. The man starts to laugh then signals
to a group of friends.

JAMAICAN MAN White boy says his granddaddy black.

LYSANDER His friends' start laughing too. I'm really starting
to panic now... But then...

*We hear **"GIRLS JUST WANNA HAVE FUN"** by Cyndi
Lauper.**

LYSANDER Cyndi Lauper's "Girls Just Wanna Have Fun"
suddenly blasts out of the sound system. And everyone
goes fucking nuts. It's a surreal sight as Rastas, old
ladies, Asians and the young buff teens all bump and
grind to this eighties classic. The guy in the bright shirt
smiles at me and I suddenly don't feel so scared anymore.

LYSANDER *spots something.*

And that's when I see mum and grandad. At the top of an
alleyway further up the street. Talking. Finally. It looks
like they're getting on. They hug then Grandad turns
and heads back to the party. Mum watches him go for
a second, lets out a sigh... then walks up the alleyway,
disappearing into the dark. I follow her.

*We now see some street art painted on the wall. It's a
young Jamaican boy staring out to sea. It's faded but still
quite striking.* **MARY** *is stood staring at it.* **LYSANDER**
comes up behind her.

LYSANDER Mum?

She turns and looks at him.

---

* A licence to produce WHITEWASH does not include a performance licence for
"GIRLS JUST WANNA HAVE FUN". For further information, please see Music
Use Note on page v.

MARY Hey darling. You ok?

LYSANDER Yeah. You ok?

MARY Yeah...

LYSANDER You spoke to grandad? How was it?

Beat.

MARY It was... fine.

LYSANDER Fine?

MARY Yeah... He said he was sorry. Sorry that he never came to England to see us and... That he never stopped thinking about me and... Well that he was glad that we are here to make up for lost time.

LYSANDER That's good right?

MARY Yeah... All the right things. *(Pause)* I dunno... I've thought about him my whole life... I've thought about coming here and... I thought seeing him would... Make me feel... I've never felt like I belong in England. I've lived in London my whole life... and I have nothing to show for it. I haven't made a mark. I can't sell my art. I don't own anything. I don't even have my memories because anywhere they've taken place is gone or bulldozed. And here... Well here I feel more connected, but it still doesn't feel like home... I hoped it would, but it doesn't... but... then there's you.

She looks at him.

I'm not gonna lie Lysander... Since day one the whole world has told us we're different. That I can't be your mother and... For a while it made me feel even more disconnected but now... I've realised that... you're my connection. You're my mark.

Beat.

LYSANDER No pressure then.

She smiles and turns back to the wall.

MARY What do you think of this painting?

He goes up beside her.

LYSANDER It's cool.

MARY Yeah it is.

#12

LYSANDER *stands waiting and checking his phone.*

LYSANDER Does any human in the world have more power than a drug dealer at five in the morning? They have their own perception of time. I've come outside three times now cause he's said he's a minute away and each time nada. No sign of the fucker.

He checks his phone. Then writes a text.

Hey man. Sorry to pester but how long you reckon? No kiss.

Back to the audience.

I couldn't sleep. Ruby's staying with her parents in the country tonight and... I found a gram in my coat pocket and I've accidentally stayed up all night... I definitely can't sleep now so my only choice is to get another. Where is that fucker?!

His phone beeps. He looks at it.

Blue Fiat.

He looks around then spots the car. He gets in.

Hey man?

JON Safe.

LYSANDER My dealer is called Jon.

JON *(to the audience)* I'm not.

LYSANDER He's a white guy about my age. He charges £90 a gram but eight times out of ten it's pretty solid stuff. He's knows I'm good business, so he gives me his first cut. Not mixed with too much.

JON I don't.

LYSANDER *(to JON)* Two please. Thanks.

LYSANDER *goes to leave then:*

Where are you from?

JON What?

LYSANDER I mean... I don't want to make any assumptions but... Well I'm assuming you grew up in a well...some kind of social housing right? And I was just wondering do you think /that

JON /Look man I don't wanna be rude but... Two nights ago I had to sit and listen to this fat jowly Eton motherfucker recite some poem for twenty mins, about the British Empire or something. I mean... Twenty minutes motherfucker. It was murder. All you coked up posh guys wanna run something by me you know? And I take it you know. Usually I'm like its part of the business but not tonight man... I gotta see my girl. *(Beat)* Sorry.

LYSANDER No no I'm not posh and... I'm not white.

Pause.

JON What?

LYSANDER Well my mum's black... Well mixed-raced.

JON It's dual heritage, man.

LYSANDER Sure. Sorry.

JON So?

LYSANDER So, I'm just saying... I grew up poor. We've got more in common than you /think

JON /Bruv we've got nothing in common. Absolutely nothing.

LYSANDER *looks annoyed. He's about to get out of the car then stops.*

LYSANDER I buy a lot of drugs off you.

JON I'm aware.

LYSANDER I've recommended a lot of people to you too.

JON Thanks.

LYSANDER So don't... Well don't you think...as I'm a loyal customer that you should be a bit nicer to me.

Pause. **JON** *looks at him.*

JON You get what I do, right? You get what this is? I'm a drug dealer. I deal drugs. Sure your only experience is when you come and sit in my car and waffle on for five seconds but... One of my boys got stabbed the other week cause he was set up in a bad deal. We're dodging the cops, the gangs and the other fucking drug dealers. This city is a death trap for us. But it's how we make our money. Do you know how many drop offs me and my boys are gonna make tonight? Thirty six. And I've only got three cars on. Even if we only sold one g on each drop, I'm coming back with over three thousand pounds and usually we sell double that to dicks like you so if you think I need to grin and smile at you like I work in fucking Lidl then you're fucking wrong. You see that's the beautiful thing about drugs. You need me more than I need you. Now fuck off.

LYSANDER *gets out of the car and it drives off. He stands a little annoyed and embarrassed.*

LYSANDER *does a bump of coke and turns to* LILLY.

LYSANDER Hello Lilly?

LILLY Wow. You look like shit.

LYSANDER Thanks.

LILLY *(calling back into the house)* Danny you better turn that fucking PlayStation off, I swear!

LYSANDER Can I come in?

LILLY One sec...

She stands there listening for a second then.

LILLY *(calling off)* I can still hear it Danny!

Then she gestures for LYSANDER *to come in.*

LYSANDER Wow this place hasn't changed.

LILLY Is that a joke? It's completely different.

LYSANDER Sorry... Yeah. I meant the vibe's the same.

Beat.

I was sorry to hear about you dad.

LILLY Yeah well...

LYSANDER How's your mum?

LILLY She's seen better days.

Pause.

LYSANDER And you have a kid?

LILLY Two. One's round his mates and Danny's *(calling off again)* A PAIN IN MY NECK! You better be getting ready Danny! *(back to* LYSANDER*)* He's seeing his dad today. What do you want?

LYSANDER Well...

He suddenly stumbles and steadies himself on the table.

LILLY Woah! You ok?

LYSANDER Yeah. I just...

She helps him sit.

I haven't been sleeping well recently.

LILLY You want some water?

LYSANDER No, I'm fine. Sorry...

LILLY You sure I can't get you anything?

LYSANDER Yeah. I feel better already.

LILLY You been drinking?

LYSANDER A bit.

LILLY And something a little stronger?

Beat.

I mean, your pupils are literally saucers.

LYSANDER Yeah sorry... I should go...

He gets up to leave but stumbles again.

LILLY Jesus! How big a night was it?

LYSANDER Not big, I...

LILLY What's going on?

LYSANDER What?

LILLY Well you've turned up at my door at ten in the morning spangled off your tits, so I'm guessing something's up?

LYSANDER I just... I just can't stop thinking about her.

LILLY Who?

LYSANDER Mum. Ever since I've come back here I can't. Everything has just come flooding back and I keep seeing her...

LILLY Well I'm not surprised.

Pause.

She was a good person your mum. Fucking talented. Remember that painting she did outside?

LYSANDER Yeah.

LILLY Was sad when the government painted over that. She had a tough time of it really.

LYSANDER She was convinced that Emma from number forty-six had put a curse on her.

LILLY I wouldn't be surprised. Emma was a racist fucking bitch.

They both smile.

I never really saw you after the funeral.

LYSANDER I went to stay with my second cousin. On my grandma's side. He lived up in East Finchley. Then I went to uni...

LILLY Must have been tough.

LYSANDER I can't even remember the first few years after but...

LILLY It gets easier. But stays hard.

LYSANDER Yeah.

Beat.

How about you?

LILLY Well I was married to a lord for a few years. Big mansion in the country then... Got bored and came back here.

LYSANDER Really?!

LILLY *smiles.*

LILLY I went uni and then went into social work. Met a hot bloke and we lived together for a few years. Had our boys then we broke up. Dad died and I moved back here to care for mum. That was nine years ago.

LYSANDER I'm sorry.

LILLY For what? I like it here.

LYSANDER Right.

LILLY You got any kids?

LYSANDER Soon.

LILLY No way.

LYSANDER Yeah.

LILLY The first is...nuts.

LYSANDER So I hear.

LILLY You're with the mother, right?

LYSANDER Yeah... Yeah we're together.

LILLY Cool... I thought this... Whatever this is was maybe to do with that.

LILLY No... *(pause)* We have to do a total refurbishment of the flats, Lilly.

LILLY'*s silent.*

You'll have to move off the estate for a while, but I guarantee you'll be coming back.

LILLY *still doesn't say anything.*

It's the only way /to

LILLY /So you're demolishing it?

Pause.

LYSANDER Yes, but we'll be turning it into state of the art
new /flats

LILLY No.

LYSANDER I'm sorry. I know I said /we

LILLY No! I'm not going to let that happen.

LYSANDER I've looked at all the options and this is the only
way to make sure Culross stays social housing.

LILLY But there's one fucking option you've totally forgotten.
Fighting!

Pause.

LYSANDER I am fighting Lilly. I have been fighting but... This
is what killed my mother! It's a losing battle... you have to
compromise.

LILLY No. This is my home. My family home.

LYSANDER We'll move you somewhere close. And I promise
you'll be able to come back.

LILLY Come back to what?

LYSANDER The newly regenerated /Culross

LILLY /A disgusting building designed by some dickhead with
separate doors for the rich and poor?

LYSANDER I've overseen the plans it's not /going

LILLY /How much money are you making from this?

LYSANDER *doesn't say anything.*

LILLY You've sold us out. You've used your connection... You've
used her to make this happen.

LYSANDER No.

LILLY She'd be so ashamed of... you. Have you thought about
that? She'd fucking hate you for this.... You've turned into
the very thing that killed her.

LYSANDER This place killed her! Trying to hold onto it killed her. And having to battle all the shit this city kept throwing at her. *(pause)* Aren't you sick of this? Constantly worrying about when they are going to whip this out from under your feet. Cause it was always coming. From day one. And all I'm doing is making sure it happens on our terms. So, there's something left. Because marching around with a few placards or getting your photo in the local paper does fuck all! They are coming for this place Lilly. And you need to be smart here. If you want to hold on to any part of land in this fucking city then you need to listen to me. Fighting isn't the way. We have to play the system.

LILLY The system? Is that the system that's already destroyed most of the estates in this city? The system that let Grenfell happen? The system that's now using Grenfell as an excuse to tear down more homes? The system that keeps taking away our rights? That's sending your people back to Jamaica? That system? Listen to yourself. You just think like them now. You're not playing the system, you're part of it.

LYSANDER The only way to play they system is to be part of it!

LILLY But at what cost?! You've been away from this place too long. You've forgotten who you are? Where you're from.

LYSANDER And where am I from Lilly? Cause I don't really feel like I'm from anywhere? I never have. I'm white but... I'm not. And I'm not black and... And I might have called this place home once, but it never really felt like it. I've never known where I fit.

LILLY What? So because you're having an identity crisis you don't give a shit about the people you grew up with?

LYSANDER No that's not...

Pause. LYSANDER *calms himself.*

This is the only way, Lilly. You have to believe me.

LILLY Believe you? Ha! Ok. I tell you what, I'll leave Culross but only if you tell me the truth. Only if you look me in the eye and admit that this has nothing to do with saving this place and everything to do with making money.

LYSANDER That's not true!

LILLY I'm sick of the bullshit. I'm sick of people thinking we're stupid. You have the power. You're gonna do whatever you like anyway so at least give me the decency of the telling me the truth.

Pause.

LYSANDER I... I don't know what to say.

LILLY Just say that you're out for yourself. That you need to look after number one. That deep down you believe that your needs are more important than mine.

Silence.

Just say it.

LYSANDER No!

Beat.

LILLY You're a coward, Lysander. And you know what? It's your actions that make you white Lysander, not your skin colour.

MARY I feel calm... And confident. Since we got back from Jamaica, I've felt... more in myself and most importantly... inspired. Really inspired.

MARY *goes over to the wall with a bucket of paint.*

There's a huge wall on the side of Culross that has no windows or doors on it. I think it used to be the inside wall of a wooden shed where the builders stored their tools but now... Well now it's just a big huge blank wall that makes the perfect canvas.

She starts painting on the wall.

LYSANDER It was about four o'clock on a warm Sunday afternoon and I was four hours deep into a hardcore N64 session. That's right... Zelda. I heard the front door go a while ago but just assumed mum had gone to the shops. But I'm starting to get hungry so go through to the kitchen. Mum isn't back yet but the door is on the latch. I head out onto the street. The sunlight blinds me as haven't left the house today. Then further up the road I see her... She's cleaning the side of the building... No wait... She's painting...

MARY *stops painting and stands back. It's a massive picture of her hugging* **LYSANDER**. *It's wonderful.*

LYSANDER *comes up behind her.*

Mum?

She looks at him.

MUM What do you think?

LYSANDER Is that us?

MUM Yep.

LYSANDER I... I like it...but won't you get in trouble?

MARY Probably.

They both stare at it a minute.

LYSANDER My head looks a bit big.

MARY So, it's accurate then.

LYSANDER Well you didn't paint yourself any wrinkles.

MARY Fuck off.

They both smile.

LYSANDER But then her face goes pale. She sees something over my shoulder. I turn and look.

He turns.

MARY The sun bounces off his shiny head and leather jacket –

LYSANDER – A bald man stumbling up the street –

MARY – He must be drunk. His DM boots scrape across the floor, like an Aryan zombie.

LYSANDER And then I realise. He's a skinhead.

MARY There was another National Front march in Camden today and he must have got lost... Or he's just out looking for a fight. The boots stop. He's seen me.

LYSANDER Mum let's go.

MARY *(To* LYSANDER*)* Go to the other side of the road. He can't know we're together.

LYSANDER What?

MARY Do as I say!

LYSANDER No I –

MARY – He starts stumbling towards us. *(Back to* LYSANDER*)* If he thinks we're together then it will be worse! Just walk on the other side of the road.

LYSANDER No! The DM's scrape, scrape, scrape.

MARY DO IT! Whatever happens keep walking. Don't look back. And don't say you are my son!

Beat.

LYSANDER I cross the road just as the skinhead reaches mum and stares at the painting.

MARY He's bleary eyed and woozy.

SKINHEAD What the fuck you doing painting on our fucking walls you fucking –

MARY – His breath stinks. He starts throwing racial abuse at me. Nothing I haven't heard before.

LYSANDER I stumble backwards into a nearby alley and watch.

MARY I stare the skinhead down.

LYSANDER He points at the painting and shouts. I've heard the N word before, but never in such quick succession –

MARY – But I'm not scared. He just looks pathetic to me. Like a pathetic child.

LYSANDER Mum isn't flinching and this is throwing the skinhead off. He feeds on fear and there doesn't seem to be any fear here.

MARY He moves closer but I don't blink –

LYSANDER – I want to run to her but my feet are glued to the ground –

MARY – And then I see his hands are shaking and I realise he's scared. I suddenly step towards him and he falls backwards –

LYSANDER – He falls to the ground!

MARY He scrambles back to his feet and looks at me.

LYSANDER He stares at her. His face is red now.

MARY Then he spits on the painting, shouts one last slur and shuffles off.

Pause.

LYSANDER I always remember that day. My mother standing powerful and strong and me hiding like a coward.

MARY *turns to him.*

MARY That's what you remember?

LYSANDER What?

MARY I always remember it as the day I painted that painting. The painting that outlived me.

Beat.

LYSANDER Mum died five years later.

MARY A heart attack.

LYSANDER Outside the WHSmiths by the station.

MARY The glamour.

LYSANDER She was forty-one.

MARY I was buying some interiors magazines and got in a row with the security guard who thought I was shoplifting.

LYSANDER She collapsed and… well… They said it was quick.

MARY Hope that security guard feels guilty as fuck now.

The painting on the wall starts to disappear.

LYSANDER The council painted over her painting six month later.

MARY Bastards.

LYSANDER And just like that she was gone.

They watch as the painting completely vanishes.

I'm sorry

MARY For what?

LYSANDER For everything. And I should have stood by you...
I should have stood by your that day with the skinhead...

MARY No you shouldn't have. Not that day.

She goes over to him.

But you need to remember, Lysander, that just because you
can walk away doesn't mean you always should.

#15

MARY *and* LYSANDER *go to either side of the stage.*

MARY Camden. 2020. And it is hot.

We see images of modern-day Camden and it's all shiny, white shop fronts and tourists.

LYSANDER Record levels of hot.

MARY That kind of heat that makes you feel like it's the end of the world.

LYSANDER Until it suddenly rains again. The streets are busy but calm.

MARY Tourists and shoppers weaving in and out of each other.

LYSANDER Taking pictures –

MARY – And buying mass produced tat.

We see some mass produced tat.

LYSANDER Music drifts from clothes shop doorways.

MARY Non offensive pop –

LYSANDER – And sanitised hip-hop.

MARY A man pushes an oversized pram through the busy streets. He's tall bearded and in his mid-thirties –

LYSANDER – Early thirties!

MARY And basically, the very definition of an average middle-class white man.

LYSANDER Or so he seems.

MARY He's in expensive skinny fit jeans –

LYSANDER – A gift from my wife.

MARY And a bright Burberry shirt –

LYSANDER – A gift from himself.

MARY His name is Lysander.

LYSANDER His mother was an artist.

MARY And he's seems calm and relaxed as he sips on an iced coffee purchased at an organic coffee shop.

LYSANDER His daughter gurgles.

MARY Now his daughter. His one-year-old daughter is pure delight.

LYSANDER She's a mass of curly blonde hair and bright shining blue eyes. Her name's Mary.

MARY After her grandmother.

LYSANDER And she's so cute that when Lysander is out and about with her people always stop and stare. Usually white mums –

MARY – It's always white mums –

LYSANDER – Who stop and say –

MARY – oh my god she's stunning.

LYSANDER Or –

MARY – She's going to be a model.

LYSANDER And sometimes they even flirt with him.

MARY But right now, something has caught baby Mary's eye in a shop window.

LYSANDER A large dolphin teddy.

MARY In an overpriced toy store.

LYSANDER She coos and smiles at it.

MARY And her father can't help but go inside and purchase it for her.

LYSANDER Why not?

MARY It was forty fucking quid!

LYSANDER They walk on and from where we're looking right now they look picture perfect.

MARY But they've also caught someone else's attention. A police officer.

LYSANDER A young police officer who's white.

MARY He watches them with intrigue.

LYSANDER At least we think it's intrigue. We won't spend enough time with this character to really know what makes him tick.

MARY But he's a police officer in England so it's probably a cocktail of cocaine, hatred and Ed Sheeran.

We hear an Ed Sheeran lyric.*

LYSANDER The officer approaches them –

MARY – And Lysander slows down a bit.

LYSANDER The policeman stops in front of them and looks down at the pram.

Pause.

POLICE OFFICER Awwww she's a right little trouble maker isn't she.

LYSANDER Um...yeah.

MARY And with that the policeman smiles and walks on.

LYSANDER For some reason Lysander breathes a sigh of relief.

MARY Father and daughter continue to walk. Past Camden and turning at Mornington Crescent –

LYSANDER – They head down the river towards the King's Cross regeneration.

MARY It's such a beautiful day.

---

* A licence to produce WHITEWASH does not include a performance licence for Ed Sheeran's music. For further information, please see Music Use Note on page v.

LYSANDER They arrive at St Martins and cross the small bridge.

MARY Then they cross the road and turn a corner –

LYSANDER – And that's when he sees it.

MARY The last bit of Culross.

LYSANDER A wall.

MARY The wall.

LYSANDER And behind it is a building site. Culross is gone and something new is rising in it's place.

MARY The wall is painted white.

LYSANDER Lysander looks at it.

MARY Somewhere behind all that paint is her picture.

LYSANDER He can still see it.

MARY But he'll never see it again.

LYSANDER Mary gurgles and hugs her dolphin.

MARY Lysander thinks it's time to go home. He looks up at the wall one last time. Turns the pram...and walks away.

LYSANDER *walks away from* **MARY**.

MARY *stands and watches him go.*

We start to hear **"CHASE THE DEVIL"** *by Max Romeo, The Upsetters.**

Then we see a building crumble.

Blackout.

COSTUME

MARY - ripped jeans and a faded David Bowie T-shirt
LYSANDER - skinny fit jeans and a blazer

PROPERTY

Phone (LYSANDER)	p.21
New set of building plans	p.32
Phone (LYSANDER)	p.48
Coke (LYSANDER)	p.51
Bucket of paint (MARY)	p.58

SOUND EFFECTS

Muffled reggae beat, like it's coming from next door	p.1
Music becomes louder	p.2
Phil Collins drum solo	p.4
A radio crackle	p.5
Chillout dub music	p.23
Loud drum & bass music	p.23
"OUT OF SPACE" by The Prodigy begins to play	p.28
Ska music plays and builds	p.35
Ska song plays and fades into "I DON'T CARE" by Justin Bieber and Ed Sheeran	p.36
Reggae music plays	p.40
"GIRLS JUST WANNA HAVE FUN" by Cyndi Lauper plays	p.45
Phone beeps	p.48
Ed Sheeran lyric	p.65
"CHASE THE DEVIL" by Max Romeo, The Upsetters begins to play	p.66

VISUAL EFFECTS

Images of Camden in the eighties on the wall. Punks smoking on corners, stylish black couples near Woolworths and Mods walking down the market...	p.2
An image of the strawberry Funny Feet ice cream.	p.3
A clip of the Castle Greyskull advert.	p.3
An image for a company called Four Walls projected on the back wall.	p.7

Lightning Source UK Ltd.
Milton Keynes UK
UKHW010029270619
345097UK00006B/268/P

VISIT THE SAMUEL FRENCH BOOKSHOP AT THE ROYAL COURT THEATRE

Browse plays and theatre books, get expert advice and enjoy a coffee

Samuel French Bookshop
Royal Court Theatre
Sloane Square
London
SW1W 8AS
020 7565 5024

Shop from thousands of titles on our website

 samuelfrench.co.uk

 samuelfrenchltd

 samuel french uk